WITHDRAWN

LIGHT

LIGHT

Color and Life for the World

Frederick C. Huber

DAVID McKAY COMPANY, INC. / NEW YORK

COPYRIGHT © 1978 BY FREDERICK C. HUBER
ALL RIGHTS RESERVED, INCLUDING THE RIGHT TO
REPRODUCE THIS BOOK, OR PARTS THEREOF, IN ANY
FORM, EXCEPT FOR THE INCLUSION OF BRIEF QUOTATIONS
IN A REVIEW.

Rendering of "Prism Bending White Light," and line drawings by Jack C. Wright. Nursery photo courtesy of Brooklyn-Cumberland Hospital; Saturn V photo courtesy of National Aeronautics and Space Administration; Tufted Puffin photo courtesy of The New York Zoological Park, Bronx, N.Y.; Antique Light Sources, "Tools That Made Light," courtesy of The Duro-Test Light Center, New York, N.Y.; Xenon bulb photo courtesy of Duro-Test Corporation; Hamster laboratory photo courtesy of I.M. Sharon, D.D.S. Nurse Judith Ward photo courtesy of Judith Ward.

Library of Congress Cataloging in Publication Data

Huber, Frederick C
Light, color and life for the world.

SUMMARY: Explains the physical properties of light, the sources of illumination man has used, the benefits of light in medicine, and the relationship of light to plants and pollution.
1. Light—Juvenile literature. 2. Photosynthesis—Juvenile literature. [1. Light] I. Title.
QC360.H8 535 77-14225
ISBN 0-679-20436-9

10 9 8 7 6 5 4 3 2 1

MANUFACTURED IN THE UNITED STATES OF AMERICA

To Joanne, John,
and Ronnie

Contents

LIGHT

1 / *Light Colors the World*

Look around you. Everything you see—this book, the walls, the people near you, a building, or a tree outside your window—is reflecting light. You can see them because light lets you see. Light shines, strikes an object, and reflects into your eyes. You see the object.

Without light, you can see nothing. In a completely dark room you see no shapes, no forms, no colors. This is because there is no light to reflect off objects and into your eyes.

Now look at the colors of the things around you. All the colors you see—the red, yellow, and violet shades of flowers; the green of grass; the vivid blue of a jay; the pink, tan, brown, yellow or black tones of your skin; all the colors in your world, in fact—are reflections of the colors in the light that shines on them.

Light comes to you in *waves,* or beams of energy. The light waves coming to the earth from the sun range from very short waves to very long waves. Extremely short waves and long waves of light are invisible to you, but in between them are waves of light that you can see when they reflect off the objects around you. These are the colors of the visible waves: violet, blue, green, yellow, orange, and red—the light that colors our world.

We call all the light from the sun, both the invisible light and the visible light, one word: *spectrum.* The invisible part of the spectrum lies at either end of the colors you can see. Figure 1 shows how the sunlight spectrum is divided.

The whole sunlight spectrum supplies warmth, but infrared energy (at the far right of Figure 1) gives us *only* heat, the same heat that melts snow on pleasant winter days and that starts new plant growth in early spring. The sun's spectrum, including infrared energy, is the warming force that allows all life on earth to exist.

Ultraviolet energy (at the left of Figure 1) is much more mysterious. It affects you and every plant and animal in a way not yet fully understood. Nearly every scientist and engineer who has studied light believes that ultraviolet energy is necessary for living things, but they are not sure exactly why or how ultraviolet energy is so important. Life, both plant and animal, has developed through the centuries under sunlight, including

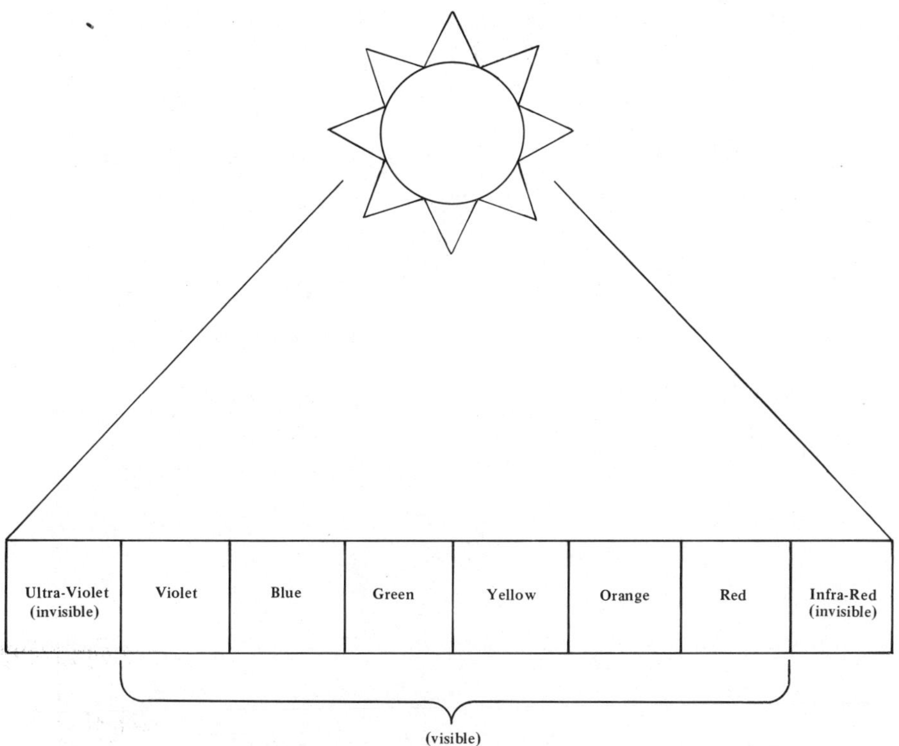

Figure 1

ultraviolet. So ultraviolet is both important and beneficial. But, just as surely, scientists have learned that too much ultraviolet can be harmful to human beings. For instance, if you receive too much ultraviolet, it can cause damage to your skin; it can cause a type of blindness; and it may even cause skin cancer.

However, just the right amount of ultraviolet from the sun is essential to life. It helps your body manufacture vitamin D, for example. And vitamin D, in turn, helps your body use calcium, a chemical that makes your bones and teeth strong. So it is clear that you need a "balance" of ultraviolet. Too much or too little can be harmful. That necessary balance is something like your need for water. Without water, you would die of thirst. But with too much water you would drown. The proper amount of water keeps you alive and healthy. Just enough ultraviolet light does the same thing.

Besides illustrating infrared and ultraviolet light, the simple drawing of the sun's spectrum (Figure 1) shows the light that you can see—the light that colors the world. If those colors were not contained in sunlight, you would not be able to see them in anything around you.

The most important thing to remember about light and color is that *colored objects reflect only the color, or colors, of the light shining on them.* If you are to see the *real* color of anything, the light shining on that thing must contain all the colors the object will reflect. Suppose, for instance, you buy a red sweater. The first time you wear it outdoors, you may be surprised by its color. The sweater will probably be a brighter or a "redder" red than you remembered it from the store. This is not only because outdoor light is brighter than indoor light. It is also because sunlight is "more colorful" than the lights used in homes and stores. Sunlight contains all colors in almost equal amounts; the light from most light bulbs does not have equal amounts of all colors. The chances are that the store where you bought your sweater used fluorescent lights—long, thin tubes mounted in rows on the ceiling. Most fluorescent tubes give off light that contains all colors, but the amount of those colors is different from the amount of colors in sunlight. So if the light shining on the sweater in the store had too much yellow-green and not much red, the sweater would look flatter, or paler, than the vivid red it really is.

Let's take another example. Suppose you are redecorating your bedroom. You buy curtains in one store, paint in another store, and wallpaper in a third store. While you may have very carefully selected all the colors to be certain they match, you are apt to be very surprised when you have finished working on your room. During the daytime, with window light brightening the room, the colors may be different from the perfect match you believed they were. Then, at night, with a table lamp turned on, the colors may look different still. That is because all three light sources—the lights in the store, sunlight, and the bulb in the table lamp—contain different amounts of colors. And their light, reflecting off the colored things in your room, shows these colored things differently.

For this reason, remember that when you are

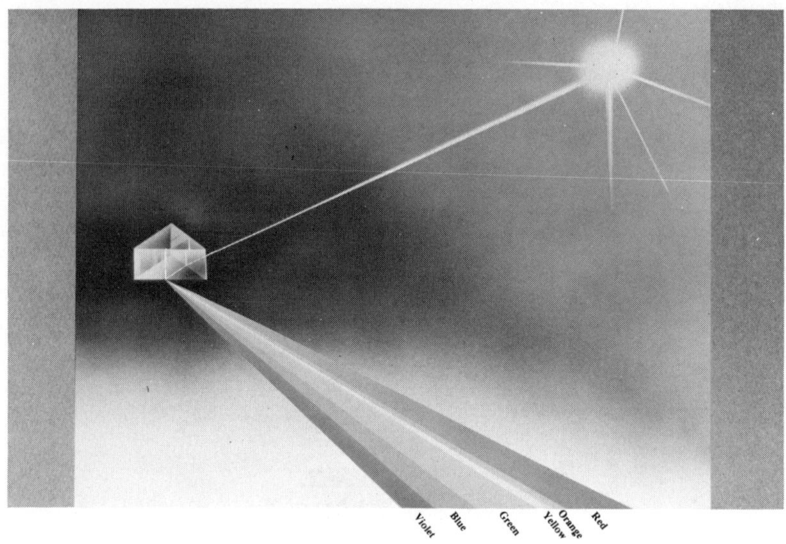

Figure 2

Although people sometimes talk about a "sunny yellow" color, sunlight is actually pure, white light. It's white because it contains equal amounts of all the colors of light that we can see: violet, blue, green, yellow, orange, and red. You can see all those colors when sunlight is "bent," as it strikes raindrops or the spray of a waterfall or a garden hose and creates a rainbow. The illustration shows sunlight's rainbow of colors—called its visible spectrum—as it strikes a piece of glass called a prism. *The colors of the rainbow are distinctly separated and labeled so that you can see where each is in the spectrum. But if you've ever seen a rainbow, you know there's really no separation; each color blends delicately into the next. The sun's reputation for being yellow, rather than its true white, probably comes from looking at it against the background of the blue sky. The sky looks blue to us because the sun's short, blue rays are scattered (reflected in all directions) by dust and vapor in the earth's atmosphere.*

shopping for things whose colors are important to you, try to look at them in the light coming through a window. Because sunlight contains all colors, you will then be able to see all the colors and their blends in the merchandise you are buying. Under sunlight you will see the *real* colors of everything.

The color difference between indoor and outdoor light may bring a pleasant, or an unpleasant, surprise when you buy a sweater or decorate a room. But the difference is even more important to many industries. People who grade food, such as meat, grains, and vegetables, need perfect light to tell the difference between good and inferior food. Most paint and dye makers use sunlight or sunlight-simulating light (artificial light that contains all colors in equal amounts) to be certain that the colors they produce are "true" every time. Artists have, for centuries, relied on the perfect colors in sunlight to reproduce on canvas the colors they see in nature. Today's printers use the same type of light to be sure that the colors they print on their presses are identical to the original photo or painting they are reproducing.

The quality of light, or its closeness to sunlight, is also very important to people who examine fibers such as raw cotton. Under sunlight they can detect even the slightest differences in the whites and off-whites of the fiber. And most dentists must rely on light with perfect color. When a dentist puts false teeth in a patient's mouth, he can very closely match the color of those teeth to the patient's remaining good teeth if he compares the false teeth and the real teeth under the true light of sunlight.

To put it simply: you do not see as well under artificial light as you do under sunlight or light that imitates sunlight. Look at a rose in sunlight, and then look at it under a light bulb. Your eyes will easily show you the difference between the colors in those two light sources. If the color is not in the light, you will not see the color in the object you are looking at. Because sunlight contains all colors, you can see all colors under sunlight. And because the world is a world of colors, you see everything better under sunlight. Your eyes and brain use the colors of objects to help identify them and to make them stand out from other objects.

2 / *The Story of Illumination—from Torch to Xenon*

Throughout history, civilizations have thought of light as a symbol of good and darkness as a symbol of evil. That is not too surprising when you remember that the earliest people had only the light of the sun to see by. During the daytime they could spot danger and flee if necessary. At night, with only faint moonlight to see by, they became easier prey for wild animals. Nighttime, without light, meant danger, cold, and fear. Dawn brought light, warmth, and safety.

Then, at some point before recorded history, early man carried a burning stick (probably from a fire started by lightning) to the mouth of his cave. Fire, once a mysterious and deadly thing to be feared, became a tool. A small fire burning all night meant warmth and safety that did not depend on the time of day. Nighttime light enabled early tribes to see predators attempting to sneak up on them, and those same predators were naturally afraid of the fire and the light it gave.

As time passed, people taught themselves how to create fire with the heat of friction, or by striking a spark to small, dry pieces of wood. Then they observed that some animal fats would burn. When a stick was coated with those fats and set afire, it flamed for a long time. Thus the torch originated.

Throughout the centuries people improved upon the light they made—from the torch to the candle to the lamp to the lantern. They experimented with fats, resins, and waxes; and with oils from plants, animals,

Figure 3. *Egyptian Closed oil lamp c. 500* B.C.

Figure 4. *Rushlight holder c. 100.*

Figure 5. *Candlejack c. 1400.*

and the ground. They lit fibers, reeds, cloth, and anything that would burn and give more and longer-lasting light after the sun had set.

As recently as 100 years ago, people still brightened nights with open flames, this time from natural gas. The gas flame was, to be sure, the best light that had been devised until then. It was cleaner-burning than a candle or oil lamp, and it did not flicker. It required little maintenance, with no wicks to buy or trim and no containers of fuel to be stored. It was convenient too; there seemed to be an endless supply of natural gas that was piped directly into homes or places of business. But gaslight was still little better than the torch or oil lamp because it was dim and also dangerous. After thousands of centuries, humanity was still lighting the hours between dusk and dawn with fire. Then in 1879 Thomas Alva Edison, a young inventor from Menlo Park, New Jersey, created the first practical electric light bulb—"a light in a bottle," a light without flame.

In the century since Edison invented the light bulb, many other types of lights have been developed, but the first invention, called an *incandescent* bulb, is still the kind most widely used. Certainly it is the kind you most easily recognize, for it is found in almost every home. The bulbs are called incandescent because they incandesce, or glow. And that is just about the only thing the

Figure 6. *Lard oil lamp c. 1850.*

Figure 7. *Upright mantle gas lamp c. 1900.*

Figure 8. *Edison's first practical lamp 1879.*

very first light bulbs did. Some light bulbs had been made before Edison's invention, but they gave a very dim light. So although they were interesting experiments, the bulbs were not bright enough to read or work by.

Edison's most important contribution toward a usable light bulb was an improved *filament*, the part of the bulb that actually makes the light.

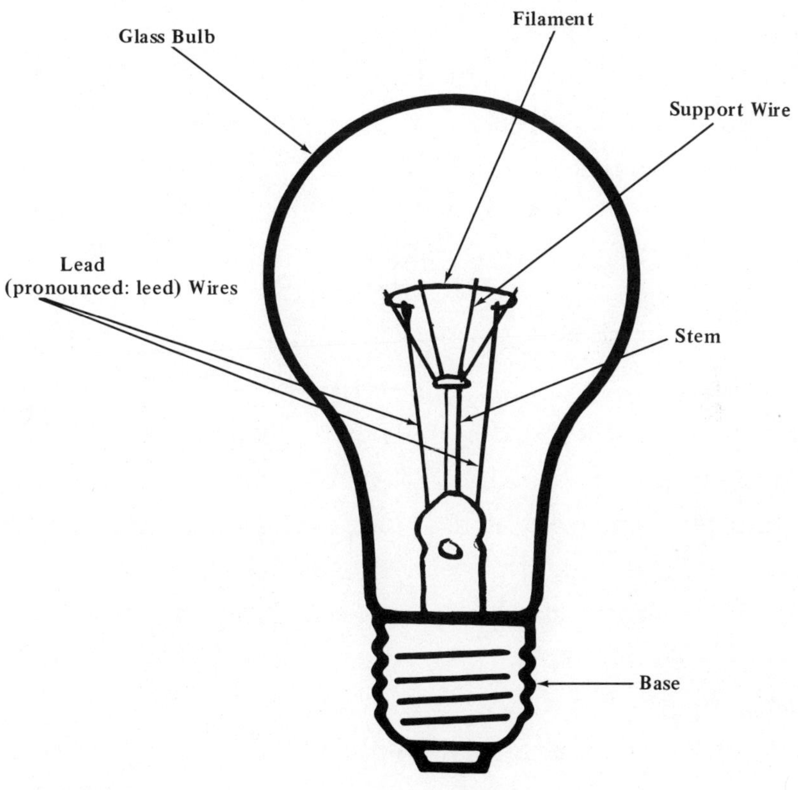

Figure 9 AN INCANDESCENT BULB

When an incandescent bulb is screwed into a socket, and the switch is turned on, electricity flows through the metal base, up through the lead wires, and through the filament. Both the base and the lead wires are made of metals through which electricity flows easily. The filament is made of a thin, coiled thread of metal that resists electricity. Although the electricity pushes its way through, the resistance causes the filament to heat up and glow. The hotter the filament becomes, the brighter it glows. That is one drawback to incandescent bulbs: most of the electricity they use becomes heat, and only ten to twelve percent of the electricity is turned into light.

Edison's very first bulb did not contain a metal filament. After experimenting with thousands of different materials, he finally had success with a cotton thread covered with carbon. But even that bulb lasted for only a few hours before it burned out, so he continued his search for the perfect filament material. He settled on hair-thin loops of pure carbon, but although these were used in bulbs for many years, they were still very fragile. Finally, in the 1920s, a way was found to make sturdy, inexpensive filaments from a metal called *tungsten*. Tungsten is still used today in incandescent bulbs.

Another kind of light bulb, the fluorescent tube, was first introduced to the general public at the New

York World's Fair in 1939. Fluorescent lights are more efficient because they give more light for less electricity than incandescents, but they have disadvantages, too. For one thing, a fluorescent requires a special fixture to snap into, a fixture not found in many homes. And a fluorescent also needs a *ballast*—a bulky, heavy device that controls the amount of electricity that enters the tube.

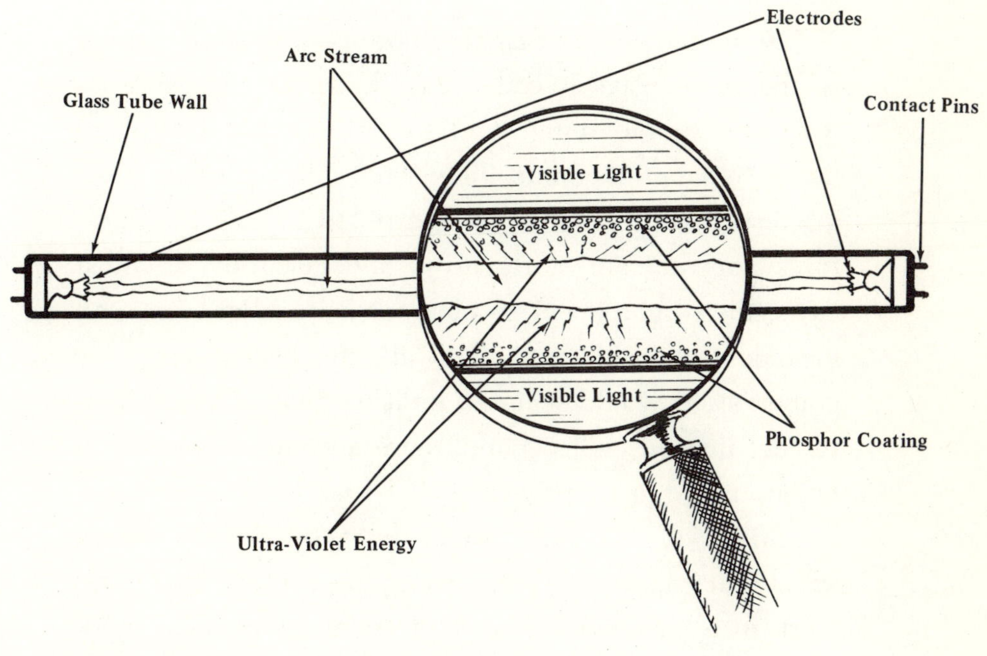

Figure 10 A FLUORESCENT BULB

A fluorescent lamp works in a much more complicated way than an incandescent. Electricity flows through the contact pins at each end and heats up the electrodes. The electrodes are covered with a coating that, when heated, creates an arc, or stream of electricity, that bounces back and forth between the electrodes. The arc changes mercury droplets into a vapor (or gas) which creates ultraviolet energy. The ultraviolet energy causes the phosphor coating (a blend of certain powdered chemicals) on the glass walls of the tube to give off light.

Some people say that the more complicated a thing is, the more ways it can break down, or not work as well as a simple thing. And sometimes that is true of fluorescent lamps. Some fluorescents flicker when they are first turned on; if they are exposed to cold temperatures, they do not start easily; and certainly, in most cases, their light is not so pleasant as the light from an incandescent bulb. But, all in all, the need for energy conservation would seem to indicate that efficient fluorescent lighting will become more and more popular in homes as the years progress.

Many of the very bright light bulbs you see in streetlights, sports stadiums, shopping centers, and gyms work in a way much like fluorescent tubes: electrodes create an arc that reacts with a gas to make light. One of the most interesting of these bulbs is one that you have probably never seen before. In fact, to look at it, you might not even think it is a light bulb.

The Xenon bulb is fascinating because it is so powerful and because its light is so white—just like the sun's. The thick, solid-tungsten electrodes are sealed in a "bubble" filled with rare xenon gas. When the arc jumps between the electrodes, the most brilliant light known is made. Because that ball of light is so hot—hot enough to melt ordinary glass—the bulb, or "envelope," is made of quartz, a clear material that is affected only

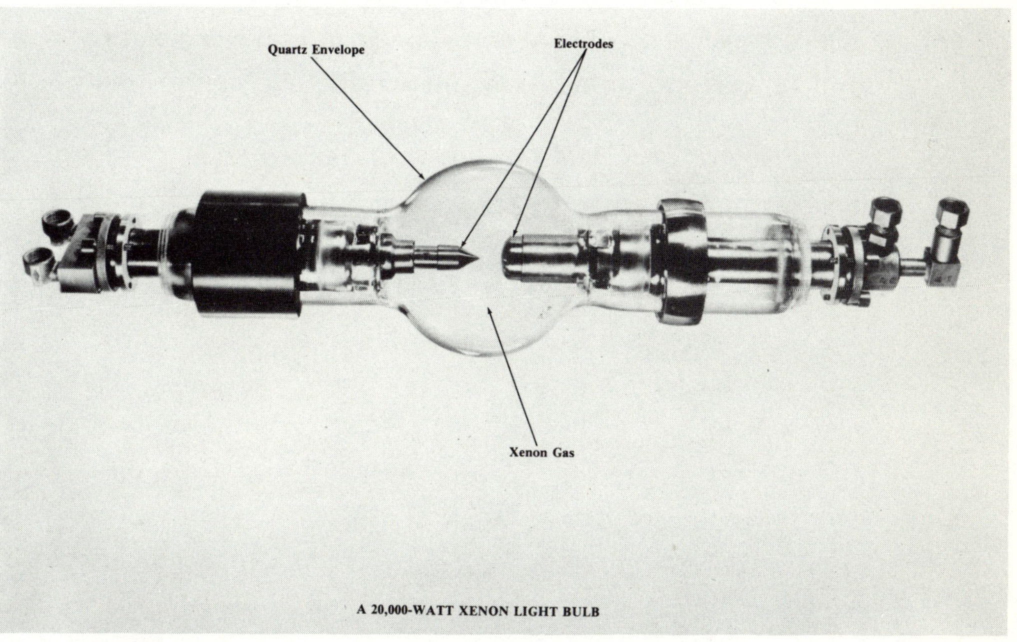

A 20,000-WATT XENON LIGHT BULB

Figure 11

by extremely high temperatures. The electrodes are cooled by air or water.

Twenty-thousand-watt * Xenon bulbs lit up the launch pads of rockets that probed deep into space and carried men to the moon. At night the intense white light of the group of Xenon bulbs made the launch pads as bright as day. The prelaunch activities could be filmed around the clock, and every detail of the count-down could be accurately observed. Because Xenon's light is so much like sunlight, these bulbs are used as solar simulators, or man-made suns, in rooms built by scientists to duplicate conditions in outer space. Just one of these Xenon bulbs is so powerful that you could read a book by its light if you were standing a mile away!

Smaller Xenon bulbs are used in the newest type of theater motion picture projectors, in extra strong searchlights on helicopters and boats, and even to light up Niagara Falls at night. It has been proposed that in years to come, the brilliant sun-like light of Xenon bulbs will be used in giant "greenhouses" to grow crops all year long.

But, as interesting as the Xenon bulb is, many lighting engineers do not think of it as the light of the future. The energy crisis and the need to conserve all

* A *watt* is the measure of the electricity used by a light bulb, or an electric motor, or an electric appliance while it is turned on.

Figure 12. *A battery of 20,000-watt Xenon bulbs illuminate a Saturn V launch vehicle during countdown before space probe.*

forms of energy and the fuels that make that energy as well, have led lighting specialists to conclude that perhaps a smaller light bulb will be the most important form of illumination in the coming years. They are convinced that a bulb that gives more light, while consuming less electricity, is what the world needs now and for a long time to come. Most manufacturers of light bulbs, in fact, have already developed lights that will do just that. And they are continuing to work on light sources that will use less electricity while they give more light.

One lighting manufacturer, working with a discovery made at the Massachusetts Institute of Technology, is developing the most efficient incandescent light bulb of all. The inside glass walls of this new light bulb will be coated with a microscopic layer of silver "sandwiched" between two layers of another material. The visible light will pass through the coating and the glass, but the heat will be bounced back to the filament. The filament will then give the light of a 100-watt light bulb while using only forty watts of electricity.

How important are more efficient light bulbs in our search to conserve energy? Well, Consolidated Edison, the company that supplies gas and electricity to New York City, estimates that 600 gallons of oil are used in a power plant to generate 1,000 watts of electricity for one year. Ten 100-watt light bulbs, if they are on all day, use up that much electricity in one year. If those ten light bulbs used just ten percent less electricity, we would save about sixty gallons of oil in a year. Now imagine the millions and millions of light bulbs used every day, and you can realize how important a more efficient light bulb would be. Light bulbs that use less electricity may very well help light the way out of the energy crisis.

3 / *Light and Plants*

Plants need light to live and grow. And you depend on plants for food. Fruits, vegetables, and grains are important sources of vitamins, minerals, and proteins—the chemicals that keep you alive and healthy. Plants are also part of the "food chain" for the animals whose meat and fish most of us eat. But plants have even more important functions than as sources of food. Without plants, you could not breathe, for all green plants manufacture oxygen, the part of the air that nourishes your body. Plants need light to produce both food and oxygen. The process is called *photosynthesis* (*photo:* light and *synthesis:* put together). Light, striking the leaves of a plant, sets a chain reaction in motion: chlorophyll (*klor*-oh-fill), the chemical that gives the plant its green color, acts on water and carbon dioxide in the plant. (Carbon dioxide is the gas you exhale when you breathe.) The water and carbon dioxide change into starches, the plant's food. Oxygen is also made in the process. Although the plant uses some oxygen, it simply releases the excess amount of that gas from its leaves.

The relationship you share with plants is very important. You inhale oxygen and exhale carbon dioxide. Plants take in carbon dioxide and give off oxygen. It is an endless cycle that is as old as the plants and animals that first shared the earth. And as long as enough green plants live, it is a cycle that guarantees a supply of oxygen for the world's billions of people to breathe.

Whatever the season, plants are welcome sights in a house or an apartment. Growing a plant in your home is not difficult at all, and after its initial purchase, costs almost nothing to maintain.

Artificial lights help plants to grow indoors in a home without a sunny window in corners away from windows. Some plants, such as the cactus, need visible and ultraviolet light to grow properly. Others, like the *bromeliads,* need ultraviolet light to bring forth beautiful flowers. Glass windowpanes block ultraviolet light, so a sunlight-simulating fluorescent tube is best for such plants.

"Plant-growth" light bulbs that screw into ordinary

Figure 13. *Some gardeners first bring seeds to seedlings (here, tomatoes and beans) with light before transplanting them outdoors.*

sockets are readily found in stores. Most of these bulbs have a pale blue coating which helps supply better light for plants than the yellow-red light given off by the filament. This combination of colored light waves is good for all the growth needs of a plant—from its seedling stage to full flowering.

Here are a few plants that a beginning indoor gardener usually can grow successfully indoors:

Jade Plant. Because the thick, round leaves of this plant soak up and store water, its soil should be left dry for several days between waterings. The potting mixture should be sandy. The plant needs sunlight or simulated sunlight about six hours daily.

Cactus. This plant needs strong sun, a warm room, and sandy soil. Be sure the soil is dry a number of days before watering; do not overwater.

Panda Plant. This cuddly-looking, fuzzy-leafed plant needs strong sun, a cool corner, and sandy soil. Water when the soil is dry.

Snake Plant, Kangaroo Vine, Pothos. These plants will do well in any light, even in dark corners. Water thoroughly, but not too often. A mature snake plant will bloom in a sunny room.

Spider Plant, Strawberry Geranium. Both of these delicately-shaped plants develop long, graceful "runners" (wiry stems) with small plants at their tips. The spider plant thrives in bright, indirect light and moist soil. The strawberry geranium likes bright sun and a cool, humid location.

Prayer Plant. Keep this plant in indirect sunlight in moderately moist soil. "Mist" it with a spray bottle once a week. At night, watch its leaves fold upward like praying hands.

4 / *Phototherapy—The Light That Cures*

Light allows you to see. It colors the world. It helps plants make the air you breathe. And light can even be used to treat or prevent certain diseases.

Treating sicknesses with light may seem like a new idea. But actually, *phototherapy (photo:* light and *therapy:* treatment) is thousands of years old. The ancient Egyptians used light to cure a kind of skin disease known as vitiligo (vit-i-*lie*-go), in which people developed white patches on their skin. The Egyptian doctors' medication? Some ointments made from herbs were first spread on a patient's skin. Then the patient was exposed to sunlight. After a time, the patches disappeared, and the skin color became normal again.

Until about 100 years ago, sick people were sometimes "treated" by sunlight, but often the treatment was accidental. Diseases were much less understood then than they are now, and doctors often prescribed medicine that would relieve the symptoms rather than cure the disease. If a sick person looked pale and weak, a doctor might prescribe a rest in the sun. Lying in the sun relieved the symptom; it made the patient look healthier as his skin reddened and tanned. And unknown to the patient or doctor, the patient was really becoming healthier because the sunlight was assisting the patient's body to fight infection by helping to manufacture a chemical, such as vitamin D, which can cure a number of ailments.

Another "accidental" use of sunlight was to disinfect the wounds of injured people and the clothes of sick people. Soldiers who were badly injured in battle often had to lie outdoors in the sun, but sometimes they recovered from their injuries more quickly than those who were brought indoors. When the clothes of people with serious diseases that could infect other people were aired in the sun, their diseases were not often transmitted to others. Sunlight played an important role in both cases because ultraviolet energy kills certain types of bacteria (one kind of germ) when it shines on an area for a certain length of time. So, with the bacteria dead, the soldiers' injuries healed cleanly and quickly, and the sick persons' clothes would not infect anyone else.

During the same time that germs became known as

disease-causers, and antiseptics were first used to sterilize operating rooms, tuberculosis was a very much feared disease. It killed thousands of people every year in many countries. Today tuberculosis is relatively easy to cure because of the discovery of "wonder drugs," such as sulfa. But in the nineteenth century those medicines were unknown, so the remedy for tuberculosis was a long rest period in sunlight, or phototherapy. And in the 1880s a Danish doctor used artificially-produced ultraviolet light to cure a type of skin cancer, a treatment still in use today.

The growth of cities in the nineteenth century contributed to a severe disease known as rickets. But light held the cure. Rickets can affect babies and children because it strikes while bones are growing. Without the proper amount of calcium, bones remain soft and bend easily so that a child cannot stand or walk properly.

How could cities cause such a disease? Because children who spent their early years in the shadows of tall buildings and in dark, narrow streets did not receive all the sunlight they should have had. Sunlight acts on a chemical in the skin to produce vitamin D which helps calcium make bones strong. Once again, the part of the sun's spectrum that stimulates the body to make vitamin D is the mysterious ultraviolet energy. So sunlight can prevent rickets and cure rickets, too.

Nowadays phototherapy is used regularly to treat diseases of the skin, such as *psoriasis*—sore and itchy scabs—and *Herpes Simplex*—small blisters that appear on the body's soft, moist tissue, such as the mouth or lips. In many cases, exposure to light containing ultraviolet energy makes these skin diseases disappear entirely.

An experiment with phototherapy seems to show us that light may cure even more severe diseases, such as *black lung*, a sickness that coal miners contract by breathing coal dust for long periods of time. One group of laboratory hamsters with black lung was exposed to ultraviolet light for one hour a day for one month, while another group was kept under ordinary light during that time. The hamsters treated with ultraviolet light were much better at the end of the experiment, while the lungs of the hamsters not exposed to ultraviolet light remained badly infected.

In Russia medical experts believe so strongly that ultraviolet light can help fight black lung that the Ministry of Health has made it a law that miners receive daily doses of that part of the sunlight spectrum. And Russian researchers have continued their study of the effects of ultraviolet light. In one experiment, workers in a machine shop were divided into two groups: one was exposed to ultraviolet light, the other was not. After six months the researchers found that the unexposed group of workers had had nearly twice as

Figure 14. *In one experiment, sun-like light helped cure hamsters such as this one suffering from "black lung" disease.*

many colds as the ultraviolet-light-treated group, and the colds were more severe.

Of all the important contributions phototherapy has made, or will make, one of its happiest applications was "discovered" over twenty years ago—a way to help the most helpless people of all, newborn infants.

In 1956, Sister Judith Ward was in charge of the premature baby unit at Rochford General Hospital in Essex, England. Along with her normal tasks, Sister Ward had taken an extra duty upon herself. On mild, sunny days she would bring some of the tiny infants outdoors where, she felt, they would benefit more from the sun and fresh air than from their stifling incubators indoors. Nearly all of "her" children suffered from *jaundice,* a disease caused by their premature birth. Because they were not yet perfectly formed internally, their bodies were unable to cleanse their blood properly. In the worst jaundice cases the babies died; in somewhat less severe cases they often suffered brain damage.

When babies are jaundiced, their skins turn a yellowish color. So Sister Ward made an exciting discovery when she changed the diapers of the jaundiced babies she had taken outdoors one warm summer day: the skin that had been covered by the diapers was yellowish, but the bare skin exposed to sunlight was a healthy pinkish white! When the hospital doctors came to examine the babies, Sister Ward told them what she had observed. The doctors were intrigued, but skeptical. Their skepticism began to vanish when they saw that other jaundiced babies exposed to sunlight were being cured, too. After the doctors had conducted careful, thorough experiments on blood samples and still more

Figure 15. *Nurse Judith Ward holding infant cured by light in England's Rochford General Hospital.*

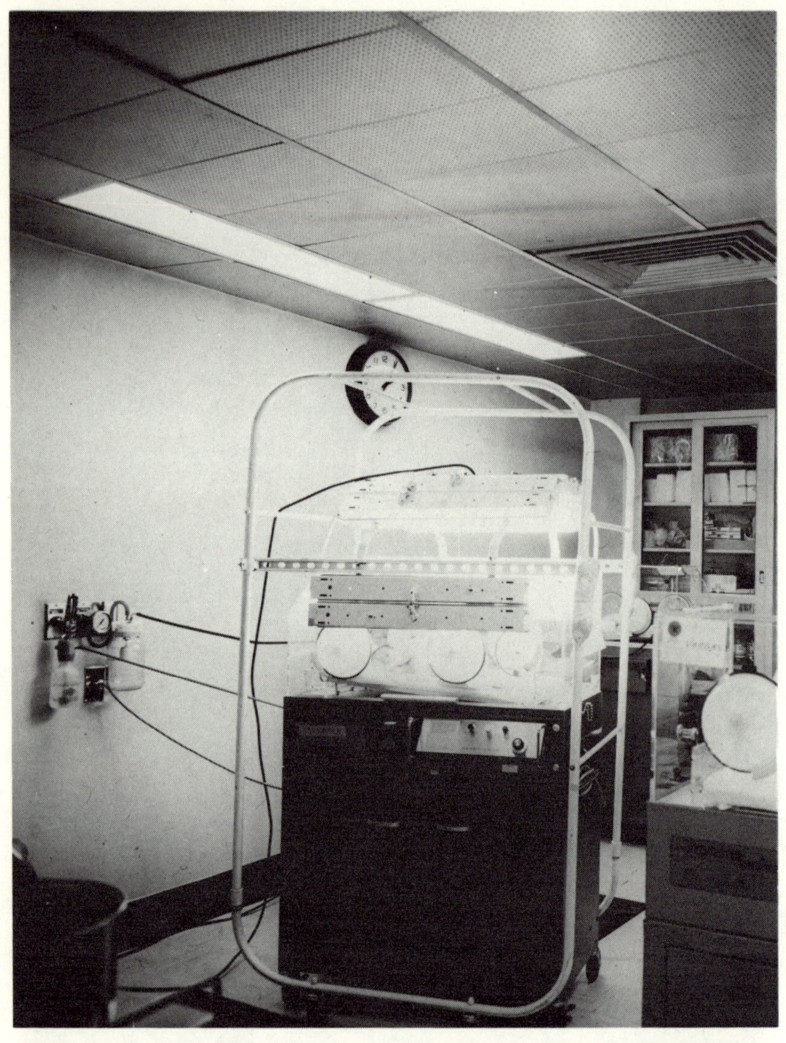

Figure 16. *Premature baby in Brooklyn-Cumberland Hospital takes a sunlight-simulating "light bath" to cure its jaundice.*

babies, they verified what Sister Ward had suspected: light could—and did—cure jaundice in infants.

Today a great many jaundiced infants, weighing only four or five pounds, bask under strong, sun-like fluorescent lights in hospital incubators. After their "light baths" they need no further treatment nor dangerous blood transfusions. Their jaundice is cured. And the cure is as safe as changing a diaper—thanks to the lights and a kind, observant nurse named Judith Ward.

5 / *Light Pollution—Good Light and Bad Light?*

Since Sister Judith Ward's discovery of a cure for jaundice in 1956, light has become the object of more and more scientific experiments. However, researchers throughout the world are just beginning to understand how and why light affects life.

Nearly everyone agrees that the right amount of sunlight is good for all of us. But now some scientists are beginning to suspect that many artificial lights may not be so beneficial. Perhaps our light, like some of our air and water, is polluted. Scientists have arrived at this conclusion through experiments with animals. In one experiment, hamsters were given foods that would make them develop cavities in their teeth. Some of the hamsters were kept under ordinary fluorescent lights,

Figure 17. *One laboratory experiment showed that golden hamsters experienced only minor tooth decay when kept under sunlight-imitating light.*

and others were kept under fluorescent lights that are very much like sunlight. At the end of the experiment, all of the first group of hamsters had many cavities, while the group kept under the sun-like light had far healthier teeth.

Zoos, too, have supplied examples of how some artificial lights may affect life in a harmful way. Not long ago workers at the Houston, Texas, Zoo thought one of their valuable snakes was dying. It would neither move nor eat. By chance the lights over its cage were replaced with the same type of sun-like light that was used in the hamster experiment. In just a few days the snake began to move about, and then ate a mouse! Examples such as these certainly do not prove that ordinary light bulbs will make people sick. But these cases, the facts about plants, and the uses of phototherapy do prove that light affects plant, animal, and human life. Sometimes the effect is good; sometimes it is bad. Remember that too much of anything is not good for you. Food, for instance, is necessary to live, but too much of any food can make you sick. And that is the way it is with light; too much can be bad, as anyone who has ever had a painful sunburn will attest.

Another example of how light affects animals involves a rare bird called the tufted puffin. Curators in the New York Zoological Park (Bronx Zoo) had carefully designed the puffins' cage to make the birds feel as if

Figure 18. *Some reptiles, such as this king snake, almost died in captivity until they were placed under sun-like light.*

Figure 19. *Tufted puffins raised a family for the first time in captivity under sun-like light in the Bronx Zoo.*

they were at home in their native habitat, the islands of the northern Pacific. But the zoologists had forgotten to duplicate one thing—sunlight. Only when their ordinary fluorescent lights were changed to sun-like fluorescent lights did the puffins develop adult feather growth. Then one puffin laid an egg that hatched. It was the first time that puffins had ever done that in captivity.

These examples point out what *can* happen to animals when they are removed from their natural surroundings, including sunlight, and put into man-made surroundings under ordinary artificial light. But examples such as these pose a question to some scientists: if animals can be harmfully affected by artificial light, can human beings be affected the same way? Is artificial light bad for us? Is it polluted? Perhaps artificial lights affect us in other ways, too. With that thought in mind, a professor at Cornell University decided to try an experiment. He observed students in a classroom studying under ordinary lights and then under sun-like lights. Each day, under each type of light, the students were tested. The professor found that the students were less tired and could see more clearly after four hours of study under sun-like light than they could under ordinary light.

In Russia an experiment also was conducted with schoolchildren. Sixth-graders were observed for a full school year. The pupils were separated into two groups.

Figure 20. *Alligators in this reptile house feel almost "at home" as they swim or bask on rocks under artificial sunlight.*

Each group's classroom was lit with ordinary fluorescent tubes. But only one group was also exposed to ultraviolet energy—the part of the sun's spectrum that is apparently so important, but missing from ordinary lights. At the end of the year the Russian scientists discovered that of the two groups, the children exposed to the ultraviolet light could see more clearly, made fewer mistakes, could work longer and better, and had higher grades. Could it be because of the light? The Russian experimenters felt sure this was so. They recommended that all schoolchildren be exposed to ultraviolet light in the same small amounts they had used in their study, or about the same amounts the children would have received if they had been outdoors under the full spectrum of sunlight.

Scientists have known for a long time that when light enters your eyes, it activates a tissue called the *retina* which is connected to the optic nerve (the large nerve at the back of each eyeball that sends the images you see to your brain). They now suspect that light signals, conducted through the optic nerve, also have an effect on the endocrine (*end*-oh-crinn) system, the glands in your body that help regulate the rest of your body by producing certain chemicals. One of these glands, the pineal (pie-*neel*), receives impulses from the optic nerve and then "tells" other glands to produce chemicals that affect the way you grow and determine when you become an adult. What does all this have to do with good light and bad light? Simply this: human beings, animals, and plants have developed through the centuries with clean air, pure water, and sunlight. But now that people have polluted the air in many places with chemicals and smoke, there has been an increase in diseases of the lungs, and many species of birds and animals have died or migrated to other areas. Where lakes and rivers have been poisoned with waste and chemicals, fish and plant life have died. For the past 100 years many people have left the sunlight and spent much of the time under artificial light that is very different from sunlight. We do not know all the effects this has brought about because researchers have only just started to investigate the possibility of light pollution.

But it is definite that the full spectrum of sunlight, including ultraviolet, is beneficial. That is certain from observing plant, animal, and human life throughout the centuries, and from the many recent studies and experiments. Perhaps light will help reduce the amount of time you spend in a dentist's chair. And perhaps some day you will take a daily "light bath" and go through a whole year without a cough or a sniffle. Those happy possibilities are something else to think about the next time you are outdoors feeling good under a pleasant, sunny sky.

DATE DUE

MAR 1 6
NOV 16 '95

D8 Fordham Equip. Co.

WITHDRAWN

19757

535
Hu Huber, Frederick C
Light; color and life for the world